Understanding
Kinesiology

Contents

Kinesiology is based on the study of the mechanics of human body movement. Over time, this has developed into the study of the body's internal communication systems, and this knowledge is used to encourage the body to restore itself to full functioning.

HOLISTIC HEALING
The work of a skilled Kinesiologist has been described as 'the most holistic therapy', as, unlike many medical specialities (general practice, dentistry, osteopathy and complementary therapies: reflexology, massage, acupuncture, homoeopathy), Kinesiology treats the whole

Kinesiology has been described as 'the most holistic therapy' person: mental, physical, and chemical.

KINESIOLOGY IN PRACTICE

The Kinesiologist uses the information from the body's own communication systems to make a diagnosis.

The scientific base of Applied Kinesiology means that treatments used by a trained Applied Kinesiologist have been rigorously tested. It is now widely accepted that the treatments are an effective method of helping the body to restore healthy functioning.

A Kinesiologist uses muscle testing to gain information about how an individual is feeling and how their body is working. The Kinesiologist interprets these muscle tests, then uses treatments that correct imbalances in the body. The result is an individual who is restored to health and well-being.

Let's consider a simple analogy. When you take your car into a garage for a service it is plugged into a diagnostic machine that receives information from all the vehicles's circuitry systems, governing fuel, air intake, coolant, brakes, suspension etc.

The mechanic matches the information against the car's optimum level of operation. The mechanic may make a few small adjustments. He knows that any adjustments made to one of the car's systems could affect others, and that all must function in harmony.

It is exactly the same with the human body – the Kinesiologist is the master mechanic.

POPULARITY GROWTH

Over the past 20 years, Applied Kinesiology has grown rapidly in popularity, and clinical research has validated many new discoveries.

'Conventional' doctors are finding muscle testing of great value. Kinesiology's system of diagnosis and treatment is based on sound principles, with feedback directly from the body. This indicates what is required to correct not only the symptom, but more importantly, the underlying cause.

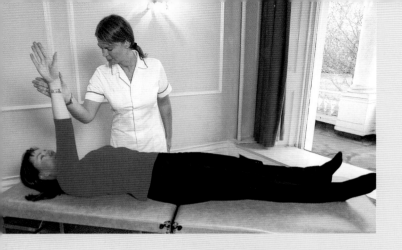

2

A Brief History

The word 'Kinesiology' has its roots in the Greek 'kenesis', meaning 'movement'. Originally, Kinesiology was the study of the mechanics of body movements.

Kinesiological structural muscle testing was first developed by the medical profession. It was used by physiotherapists and doctors to test the range of their patients' muscle movements, strength and tone, particularly in cases such as injury and stroke.

MASSAGE

Dr. George Goodheart DC was a leading chiropractor from Detroit in the USA, well known for his seminars on new techniques. In 1964, a patient was referred to him. Dr. Goodheart found severe muscle spasm.

He decided to use some structural muscle testing to check function. One of the muscles he tested was the *Fascia lata,* which runs down the outside of the leg from the hip to just below the knee. Afterwards he massaged the

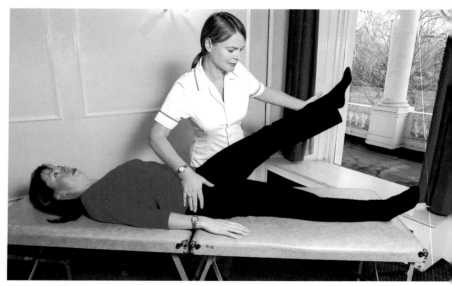

10

Testing the Fascia lata muscle.

path of the muscle and the patient reported that the pain diminished dramatically and permanently. When he retested the muscle, he found it stronger than before.

Intrigued by this, Dr. Goodheart tried to include fibre massages in his work, however he could not replicate the initial result. Then he recalled the work of osteopath Dr. Frank Chapman DO in the 1930s.

REFLEXES

Chapman had mapped various reflexes in the body that could be massaged, producing a change to the lymphatic drainage of an organ. Lymph is a fluid that feeds and cleans the tissues and intercellular spaces and is vital to healthy function.

One of Chapman's reflexes followed the identical path of the *Fascia lata*. Step by step, Dr. Goodheart matched the reflex to the muscle, and to the specific organs that they affected. These areas are now called the Neurolymphatic Reflexes.

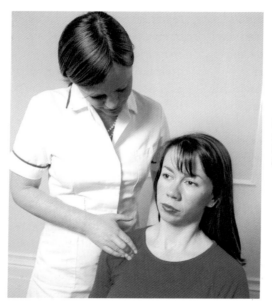

Here, the practitioner is working on the Neurolymphatic Reflexes.

The word 'neuro' implies a fast-moving electrical impulse. This term was used to explain the speed with which a massage to a point could cause an instant change in lymphatic flow, resulting in an improvement in a muscle's ability to perform.

These points are literally electrical in nature, hence their ability to create instant changes.

Dr. Goodheart's findings gained acceptance in the medical world, and soon his colleagues were adding to them.

NV POINTS

In the 1930s, chiropractor Dr. Terrence Bennett DC observed that there are areas on the head that pulse in a different rhythm to that of the blood pumped around by the heart.

These points – the Neurovascular (NV) Reflex – are the remnants of a neurological feedback mechanism in the body of the foetus. The circulation of the foetus is controlled by the blood vessels and NV points. The NV gives information to

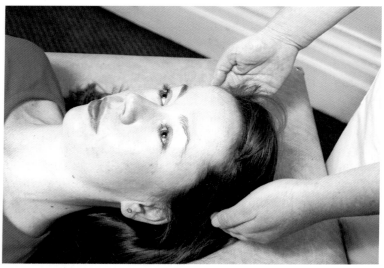

Chiropractor Dr. Terrence Bennett discovered that stimulation of the Neurovascular Reflexes in the head could improve circulation.

14

the central nervous system about the amount of additional blood needed as an area grows. After month three, the heart takes over the development of the circulatory system in the foetus.

Dr. Goodheart discovered that, after the foetal stage and on into adulthood, the NV reflexes survive on the head and some body areas. Once stimulated, these activate an immediate feedback mechanism that increases circulation to the major organs of the body. Dr. Goodheart related this information to muscle strength and weakness, and to organ function.

KINESIOLOGY AND MERIDIANS

A big leap forward in Kinesiology came after Dr. Goodheart and his colleagues proved a relationship between the eastern concepts of life force (Chi, or Prana), the pathways of energy flow in the body (meridians) and the muscles and organs.

Western medicine had traditionally disregarded the existence of meridians of energy flow, and with them the acupuncture or acupressure points that have been used in eastern medicine for more than 5,000 years.

With the use of radioactive isotopes, the 12 meridians, which lie under the surface of the skin, were traced. Their positions almost exactly matched those on the traditional Chinese charts. There were also concentrations of radioactivity at points on the meridians which corresponded to points on ancient acupuncture charts.

These meridians and acupressure points are used by Kinesiologists to restore balance and to create strong muscle-test results.

MEETING THE PUBLIC

John Thie, a colleague of Dr. Goodheart, felt that Applied Kinesiology procedures could be simplified for use by the general public. He distilled the basics of Applied Kinesiology and began teaching this to lay people. His book *Touch For Health* uses reflex stimulation methods based on the early work of Dr. Goodheart.

It should be noted that the authentic use of Kinesiology produces consistent and reliable results, and different skilled Applied Kinesiologists will usually arrive at similar conclusions when testing is carried out objectively, as dictated by their rigorous training.

Touch for Health, Balanced Health, and Systematic Kinesiology use only the techniques and methods from Applied Kinesiolgy.

DIFFERENT FORMS OF KINESIOLOGY

Health Kinesiology, BioEnergetics, and Unified BioEnergetics are names used for the practice of Kinesiology which have incorporated other methods and types of treatments.

Muscle testing is used in a variety of complementary health disciplines; for instance, it is commonly used in allergy testing.

17

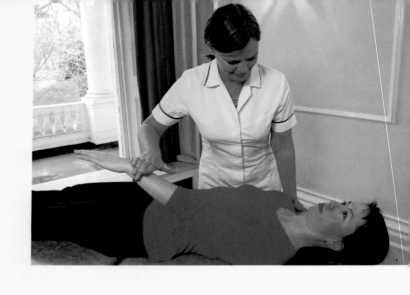

3

Body Language

Muscle testing is a method of tapping into the communication system of the whole body.

COMMUNICATION

All parts of the body are continually communicating with each other. Any change that occurs within the body will affect the whole system.

The brain acts as a bio-computer, and there are smaller bio-computers elsewhere in the body. They work together to keep track of the body's 300-plus pairs of muscles, the condition of the meridians and the organs, as well as the mental/emotional state of the person concerned.

These bio-computers also monitor the eight main body systems: cardio-vascular, muscular-skeletal, digestion, reproduction, respiratory, urinary, nervous and endocrine.

The brain is constantly adjusting, balancing and directing functions so that the body can be sustained as a self-maintaining and self-correcting mechanism.

An individual is not conscious of all this activity – it would overwhelm him or her. The bio-computers have a natural purpose: to create homeostasis, a state of equilibrium between all the interdependent elements. It is the natural inclination of the brain to correct imbalances and to restore balance to all aspects of the body.

THE TRIAD OF HEALTH

Applied Kinesiology uses the concept of The Triad of Health to describe the balance that maintains good health and well-being. The body, together with its energy system, is composed of structural, chemical and mental elements that must be equally balanced to produce the Triad of Health.

The triad is represented by an equilateral triangle with structural health (physical) as the base, and the upright sides representing chemical and mental health. All sides are held together by the energy system.

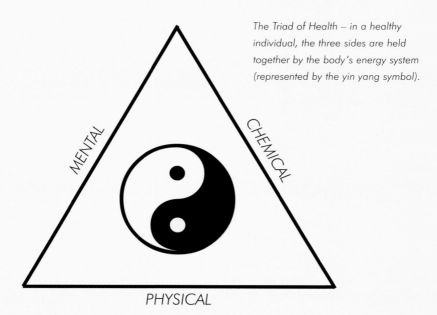

The Triad of Health – in a healthy individual, the three sides are held together by the body's energy system (represented by the yin yang symbol).

MENTAL

CHEMICAL

PHYSICAL

When a person experiences any aspect of poor health it is due to an imbalance in at least one of these elements.

- Physical: Structure, bones, muscles, tendons, ligaments posture, tone, use, fatigued, rested.
- Chemical: Air, water, diet, food, nutrition, chemical environment (pollution, chemicals, drugs).
- Mental: Thinking, reasoning, feeling, emotions, attitude, beliefs, values.
- Energy: The electrical energy of the body is composed of different systems. The meridian system is one, the aura another, Chakras and the etheric body also comprise energy. These together are said to be our Life Force, called Chi in China and Prana in India.

IMBALANCE
Someone suffering from a long term intestinal irritation will have a nutritional imbalance due to poor absorbtion of food. Long-term use of antibiotics could also contribute to this

problem. In addition, low back pain may occur due to a dual nerve supply to the lower back and to the intestine. The sufferer is likely to be mentally stressed as a result of their problem. So the victim has to put up with physical pain and mental/emotional difficulties together with a poorly performing chemical system.

Someone who is sensitive to wheat (Chemical) will often experience emotional swings (Mental), aching limbs (Physical) and loss of energy. Someone who is mentally stressed or emotionally upset may experience chemical imbalance, resulting in the physical pain of indigestion, which in turn leads to food not being absorbed correctly.

Mental stress can literally cause physical pain. The expression: "my job is a pain in the neck" is rooted in fact – people may literally experience their job stress as a pain in the neck.

REBALANCING

It is the goal of the Kinesiologist to correct the

23

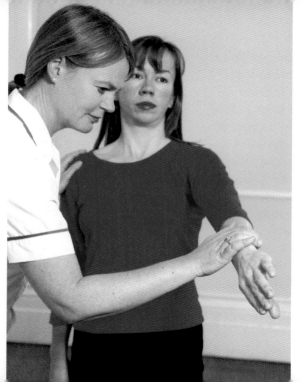

Testing the muscles helps the practitioner to diagnose an imbalance in the Triad of Health.

interplay between each side of the triangle – as a health problem on one side of the triangle can, and will, affect the other sides.

Applied Kinesiology enables the practitioner to evaluate the four factors (Chemical, Mental, Physical and Energy), and direct the therapy towards restoring the balance in the unbalanced side(s) in order to restore the Triad of Health and the energy systems.

This goal is achieved by using the system of muscle testing – tapping into the communication system of the whole body.

When a muscle is tested, the body checks with the relevant 'sub bio-computer' before responding. A strong response indicates that the 'sub bio-computer' knows that it is okay for the muscle to 'fire'. A weak response indicates that the muscle has 'switched off' and cannot function normally.

If a muscle is weak and 'switched off', it means that there is an imbalance in the Triad of Health. When the correct balance is restored the 'sub bio-computer' will receive the okay for the muscle to switch on.

This corrected, strong muscle will relay new information about its state to the 'sub bio-computer', which will in turn communicate with the whole body system.

Adjustments will then be made throughout the body. This is why seemingly simple treatments, such as a massage to a specific neuro-lymphatic reflex point, will cause a swift response. The relevant muscle will show that it has strengthened when tested again.

STRENGTH AND WEAKNESS
A muscle that 'switches on' will reprogramme the on/off switches in the rest of the bio-computers and affect their functioning, too.

In addition to injury, factors that make a muscle 'strong' or 'weak' in the terms of Kinesiology include:

• **Nutritional Needs**
  Adequate nutrition must be

available in the body for the muscles to work well. Different muscle groups need specific types of food to fuel them. Some muscles need foods rich in a particular vitamin or specific mineral in order to work properly.

- **Blood Supply**
  A good blood supply is needed to provide the muscles with oxygen and glucose, necessary to convert to energy to provide movement.

- **Lymphatic Supply and Drainage**
  The lymphatic system feeds and cleans the muscle tissues. If the lymphatic system is not operating effectively, the muscle is not fed adequately and waste products are not removed.

- **Energy Meridian**
  If the energy carried by the meridian supplying a particular muscle group is blocked, or not flowing freely, then the function will be affected

- **Mental Functioning**

  Negative thoughts can make muscles weak. In a person experiencing mental stress, a muscle can 'turn off' and test weak. For example, someone affected by mental stress can often find that their neck will hang forward and their shoulders will roll inwards.

  This is a consequence of negative thoughts inhibiting the proper working of the neck muscles.

- **Posture**

  If the body is out of alignment, muscles will be affected adversely, to a greater or lesser degree. Spinal manipulation and treatments can affect the flow and pressure of the cerebral spinal fluid that encase the nervous systems. These are treatments that Kinesiologists who also are qualified osteopaths, doctors or orthopaedic specialists will undertake.

Good (left) or bad (right) posture can have a dramatic influence on the overall health of the body.

29

4 What Kinesiology Can Help

Many people will seek out a practitioner of Applied Kinesiology when they have not been able to gain help through orthodox medical healthcare.

Others will have a health problem that they don't feel is 'bad' enough to warrant a visit to their doctor.

COMMON HEALTH PROBLEMS THAT CAN BE HELPED BY KINESIOLOGY

- Aches and pains
- Acne and eczema
- Allergies and food intolerance/sensitivity
- Anxiety, panic attacks, etc.
- Arthritis
- Asthma
- Back problems
- Behavioural problems in infancy and childhood
- Catarrh (including childhood infections such as ENT infection)
- Colds and flu

- Depression
- Diarrhoea
- Digestive problems (indigestion, nausea, flatulence, Irritable bowel syndrome, etc.)
- Dyslexia
- Eating disorders
- Exhaustion and fatigue (including ME, post viral syndrome)
- Headaches (including migraine)
- Hormone-related disorders
- Learning problems
- Menopause
- Menstrual pain
- Mood swings
- Muscular aches and pains
- Nerve root irritation
- Phobias
- Poor circulation
- Post traumatic stress
- Sleep pattern disorders (including insomnia and hypersomnia)
- Sciatica
- Stress
- Vertigo
- Weight problems (loss and gain).

Where a patient cannot be tested directly, a surrogate can be used.

Infants and the elderly, athletes and other sports people, the unwell or injured – all can benefit from Kinesiology. In the case of an infant, or if there is any other reason why direct muscle testing cannot take place, the Kinesiologist will use a surrogate (i.e. another person) who can be muscle tested while holding or touching the patient.

Kinesiology takes the view that every simple thing that happens to a person – such as falling over, eating the wrong foods, receiving a shock, being involved in an accident – can cause imbalance in the individual's Triad of Health.

These imbalances may be so minor that they have no real effect upon health or well-being. However, neglect or accumulation of these imbalances will result in 'compensations'. Compensations lead to changes in the functioning of the body, which in turn can lead to discomfort, feeling under par or being posturally out of alignment.

Most people ignore these signs, believing they will go away in their own time and that they are too minor to worry the doctor about. However, actual symptoms may arise, such as headaches, back pain, stiff shoulders, bad skin, poor digestion, or irritability.

These symptoms become persistent, and may gradually worsen. It is at this point that an individual will take the step to seek professional help. If the help given does not rebalance the individual's Triad of Health, pathological changes may occur (i.e. disease may develop). The disease and its symptoms are likely to be acute. Professional health treatment will be sought and there may be surgical or drug treatment.

An Applied Kinesiologist can tackle any result of these compensations. Even if the problem is pathological (i.e. a disease has been diagnosed), it is still possible to address the person holistically and rebalance them. This raises the individual's immune system and energy levels, and helps them to fight disease along with treatments from healthcare professionals.

Prevention is better than cure, and Kinesiology can pick up minor imbalances before they lead to compensations and functional changes. A Kinesiology practioner will be willing to help an individual to practise prevention, as well as to intervene in existing health problems. Many beneficiaries follow on with intermittent visits to their practitioner to receive balancing sessions.

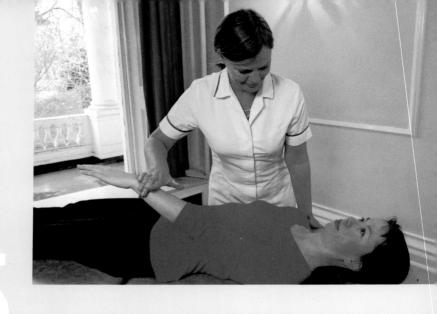

5 The Practitioner

The practitioner will discuss your case history, covering your lifestyle as well as the specific problem you are experiencing.

He or she will then start a series of diagnostic muscle tests, and there will be immediate feedback from your body when a muscle tests weak or strong.

The practitioner will then attempt to determine why a certain muscle is not functioning properly. You will be involved, as you will be aware of what is testing weak, and what is testing strong.

More questions will be asked about your everyday routines to further evaluate ways to balance the muscle weakness.

The practitioner may also wish to use standard diagnostic tests, for instance X-rays or blood tests, either via your GP or directly.

The Kinesiologist will choose the relevant technique or a combination of techniques in order to create the conditions for the muscle to strengthen and test strong.

The practitioner may make adjustments to the blood supply by touching the neuro-vascular contact points on the head, or he or she may encourage lymphatic flow by massaging the relevant neuro-lymphatic massage points. The practitioner may also stimulate along the length of certain meridians, or touch different acupuncture points on the meridians.

In order to address each circuit thoroughly, the practitioner may suggest nutritional supplements to support the body's chemistry.

He or she also may use different Kinesiological methods to help the person emotionally. Depending on a Kinesiologist's training, he or she may use other treatments, such as Bach Flower Remedies.

Through these methods, the brain and bio-computers receive new information. As adjustments are made to one aspect, the bio-computers will in turn change to accommodate the new

programmed information.
The individual's whole system will tune in and adjust to healthier functioning, moving towards good health and well-being.

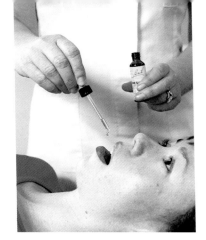

The Kinesiologist may use other forms of complementary treatments alongside Kinesiology, such as Bach Flower Remedies.

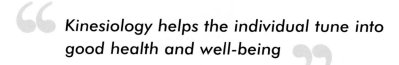

Kinesiology helps the individual tune into good health and well-being

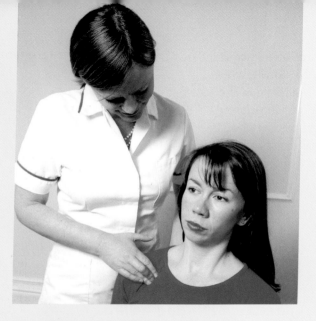

6 Case Histories

The following case studies have been complied by Stephanie Mills (Vice Principal of the Academy of Systematic Kinesiolgy).

They illustrate how a Kinesiologist works.

❶ RECURRENT HEADACHES

I had a lady in her early fifties come to see me with recurrent headaches. She had been checked out thoroughly by her GP, who could not find anything wrong with her.

When I saw her, she was extremely concerned at the frequency of the headaches (two or three times a week) and also the severity of them.

After taking a case history, I tested various muscles. It soon became apparent that many of the muscles around her neck, particularly the anterior neck flexors and the upper trapezius muscles, were not working efficiently.

This had led to tremendous tension in the back of the neck, especially around the

41

occipital area, which was affecting the flow of energy, lymph and blood supply.

A chemical factor in these weaknesses was consumption of coffee, as this was 'turning off' her neck. I balanced the muscles thoroughly, which released the tension at the back. She made some lifestyle changes, including a significant reduction in her coffee intake.

After the first treatment she felt a rush of energy. I worked on her three more times and her headaches went. She now comes for maintenance treatment about four times a year. Her headaches have never returned.

A persistent headache is just one health problem that may be treated by Kinesiology.

❷ PROLONGED LOW BACKACHE

A gentleman who had suffered from low backache for several years came to see me. He had been checked by his GP and had sought other forms of healthcare. He had experienced some help, but the back problems persisted.

He proudly told me that he never drank tea or coffee, but that he drank a lot of Coca-Cola! He never drank water. Through muscle testing it was clear that his lack of water had led to systemic dehydration –

a significant factor in his pain.

To treat the gentleman, I balanced the muscles in the front of his body, particularly the abdominals, using the neuro-lymphatic massage points. This released the tension in his back and eased the pain he was feeling. There was also an emotional element to the case – he was going through a divorce.

Our backs are very much related to supporting us, both physically and mentally, and I worked extensively with him to support him through the emotional trauma he was experiencing, using a tool called 'emotional stress release', which is extremely effective in helping people deal with mental problems. After a few sessions, his backache was 80 per cent reduced.

❸ IRRITABLE BOWEL SYNDROME

A young girl came to see me with persistent diarrhoea. Using muscle testing, I discovered that her ileo-caecal valve, the junction between the large and small intestine, was not working as efficiently as it should. This poisons the body, resulting in a plethora of seemingly unrelated symptoms, from digestive complaints to joint problems, low energy, mental confusion and headaches.

This valve is affected by what we eat, but it is also under the control of the limbic system of the brain, so is profoundly affected by emotions.

I corrected her ileo-caecal valve by working on many acupuncture points and rubbing lymphatic reflex points. I then did some food sensitivity testing and discovered that she was very sensitive to both wheat and dairy products. She had explained to me that her IBS was significantly worse during the week, and we linked it to the stress she was under at work.

By working with her diet and mental stress, and by resetting her valve, we significantly changed the severity and frequency of the diarrhoea, so that she no longer needed to plot her way across the country through the availability of toilets!

Food sensitivity testing can help to diagnose an underlying problem.

7

Self-Help Techniques

Many beneficiaries of Kinesiology find that practising at home can help them to maintain their health. Once you have visited an AK practitioner a few times, you should find that self-help techniques are relatively straightforward to learn.

TRACING THE MERIDIANS
There are 14 main meridians. Twelve of them are connected to their own organ and are bi-lateral – there is one on each side of the body. The meridians lie under the skin, and, where each meridian ends, there is an internal channel that links it to the next meridian.

The 12 meridians all run into each other and form a circular system, yet each meridian has characteristics of its own and performs a specific function for its related organ.

There are two reservoir meridians: the Central (conception) Vessel and the Governing Meridian, which run up the centre front and centre back of the body.

47

You can trace or brush meridians, which has a calming, uplifting, energising effect and feels very pleasant. Use finger tips to brush the clothes lightly in the direction of the meridian (see arrows).

Firstly, brush the Central and Governing meridians to strengthen the whole meridian system. You can also do this for yourself as part of a daily routine. Don't worry about the bit that you may miss on your back. Brush the meridians five or six times.

Then brush the other meridians two or three times each and complete the exercise with a further two or three brushes of the Central and Governing meridians.

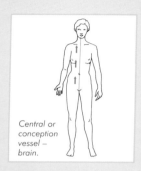

Central or conception vessel – brain.

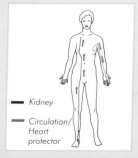

— *Kidney*

— *Circulation/ Heart protector*

ORGAN MERIDIAN ENERGY FLOW PATTERNS

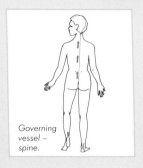

Governing
vessel –
spine.

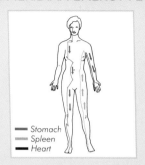

■ Stomach
■ Spleen
■ Heart

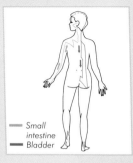

■ Small
intestine
■ Bladder

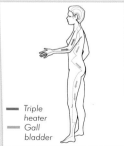

■ Triple
heater
■ Gall
bladder

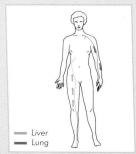

■ Liver
■ Lung

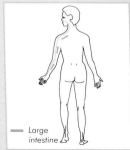

■ Large
intestine

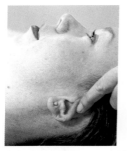  

Left: *Ears can become folded during sleep.* Centre and right: *Stretching and rolling the ears will improve energy flow and help your understanding of what you hear.*

UNFOLDING YOUR EARS

The ears receive electrical energy from outside the body. At night, people often lie on their ears and crumple them. This inhibits efficient energy flow. When the energy is not flowing freely this can affect hearing, comprehension, attention span and concentration.

As part of a daily routine it is

beneficial to unfurl the ears. It is as easy as stretching the edge of the ear outwards, with firm rolling pressure. This is good daily practice and will improve both how you hear and your understanding.

Children and adults who have been labelled as slow learners can benefit from this regular daily routine.

MENTAL ALERTNESS

This is a very simple exercise, which will help the two sides of the brain to communicate better. The left-hand side of the brain controls the right-hand side of the body, and vice versa. The two sides are connected by, and communicate through, the corpus collosum.

Spend a few minutes every day drawing lazy eights. Standing face on to the centre of the lazy eight (see page 52), follow the direction of the arrows on the illustration with your eyes. Use first one hand to draw and then the other.

You will find that the lazy-eight exercise, undertaken regularly, will improve writing, spelling and thinking. Again, it is

A few minutes spent drawing lazy eights will help your mind stay alert.

helpful for those with learning difficulties, or for those people who are affected by dyslexia.

IMPROVE BRAINPOWER AND CO-ORDINATION

Cerebo spinal fluid (CSF) bathes the brain and is vitally important to communication through the central nervous system.

CSF is part of the delicate control relationship between the brain and the body. Body movements such as those of the skull bones, ribs and pelvis, create the pumping action that is required for CSF to move around.

Stagnant CSF, through a sedentary lifestyle and/or shallow breathing, can cause co-ordination problems, hyperactivity in children, poor memory, slow learning and poor concentration. Cross Crawl exercises are a good method of pumping CSF around the body.

CROSS CRAWL
If you use a simple exercise

Cross Crawl exercises will improve your co-ordination.

53

called Cross Crawl regularly, you will find improvements in co-ordination, clearer thinking, sharpened vision, increased learning ability, enhanced strength and improved IQ amongst other benefits.

Cross Crawl is simply an exaggeration of the walking movement. If you perform 25 sets (the left arm and right leg raised and the right arm and left leg raised is equal to one set), four times each day, the benefits are experienced within a couple of days.

The Cross Crawl exercises (see pages 56-57) are also recommended by Kinesiologists for learning difficulties in both children and adults. These can be of a minor nature or severe. Cross Crawl will help to strengthen the brain/body connection.

BRAIN/BODY CONNECTIONS

The brain/body connection works best when the left hemisphere controls the right side of the body and vice versa. When this connection has not been correctly learnt, an individual will experience problems of co-ordination, thinking and learning.

The reason for this is that, at birth, and for the first year of life, the baby is homolateral – the left hemisphere of the brain controls the left side of the body, and the right hemisphere of the brain controls the right side of the body.

It is not until the baby becomes more mobile that the crossover to the contralateral (left side of the brain controlling the right side of the body and vice versa) will occur.

However, if the baby isn't allowed to crawl, uses a baby walker, or clings on to furniture to get around, the nerve pathway transition doesn't always become fully developed.

Dyslexic tendencies, poor memory, clumsiness and learning skills can be dramatically improved with regular practising of Cross Crawl exercises.

THE CROSS CRAWL EXERCISES

Follow the direction of the arrows to practise each movement.

❶

Keeping the right leg on the floor, bring the left leg and the right arm forwards, and move the left arm behind.

❷

❸

Ensure that the arm and the opposite leg move in the same direction.

❹

From a standing position, move the left leg back and the left arm forwards, and then reverse.

8

Useful Contacts

International College of Applied Kinesiology (ICAK)

This college was founded in 1975 by a group of chiropractic doctors to research Kinesiology and to teach others how to apply its techniques.

Over time, and as a result of the directed research undertaken by the ICAK, more information and techniques have been added to the original body of knowledge compiled by Dr. George Goodheart. When stringent criteria are met, new methods and applications can be incorporated into the scientific knowledge that is accepted by the International College of Applied Kinesiology. They are represented on a world-wide basis through different chapters of the ICAK.

More information can be found at: www.icakusa.com

International College of Applied Kinesiology UK (ICAK – UK)

The International College of Applied Kinesiology is a training organisation open to healthcare practitioners who are qualified in osteopathy, chiropractic,

59

medical, dentistry or veterinary medicine.

Contact The Administrator on 01403 734321

Doneechka Clinic, Mill Straight, Southwater RH13 9EY or admin@icak.co.uk Website www.icak.co.uk.

The Academy of Systematic Kinesiology (Vice Principal: Stephanie Mills)

A training organisation that trains lay people and qualified healthcare practitioners using Kinesiology methods that have been clinically ratified by the ICAK. Principal Brian Butler pioneered the use of Kinesiology in the UK and Europe. TASK. maintains a register of practitioners, both healthcare professionals and complementary health practitioners.

Contact the Academy at: 16 Iris Road, West Ewell, Epsom, Surrey KT19 9NH.
Tel: 020 8391 5988
email: info@kinesiology.co.uk
or Website:
www.kinesiology.co.uk

Kinesiology Federation

The Kinesiology Federation is an umbrella organisation representing many different Kinesiologies in the UK. Its aims are to uphold training standards, represent its members, and promote Kinesiology. It maintains a register of Kinesiologists nationwide. The Federation is working with the Sector Skills Council, a British Government organisation that are the Standards Setting Body for Health in the UK, in order to develop National Occupational Standards (NOS) in Kinesiology. These standards will assure the public of high standards of competence from their chosen practitioner. Draft standards are now in consultation.

Kinesiology Federation,
PO Box 28908, Edinburgh,
EH22 2YQ, Scotland.
Tel: 08700 113545 Monday - Thursday, 9am-12pm
(answer machine outside these hours)
Email:kfadmin@kinesiology federation.org Website:
www.kinesiologyfederation.org

About the author

Roz Collier is a writer with a special interest in those branches of complementary health that are based on sound scientific principles. A personal beneficiary from the techniques of Applied Kinesiology, she is also a clinical hypnotherapist and co-author of *Slim By Suggestion* (Thorsons). Roz has collaborated extensively for *Understanding Kinesiology* with Stephanie Mills Lic.AC, M.T.Ac.S, Vice Principal of The Academy of Systematic Kinesiology. Stephanie works in Surrey and can be contacted for treatment on 07789 437 194.

ACKNOWLEDGEMENTS
Special thanks are due to Lucinda Bligh, who modelled for the photographs. Lucinda runs her own Kinesiology clinic in London. She can be reached on 020 8510 3426 or 07984 761 330.

Other titles in the series

First published in 2004 by First Stone Publishing
PO Box 8, Lydney, Gloucestershire, GL15 6YD United Kingdom

The contents of this book are for information only and are not intended as a substitute for appropriate medical attention. The author and publishers admit no liability for any consequences arising from following any advice contained within this book. If you have any concerns about your health or medication, always consult your doctor.

ISBN 1 904439 20 9

Printed and bound in Hong Kong through Printworks International Ltd.

1

Introducing Kinesiology